AF228643

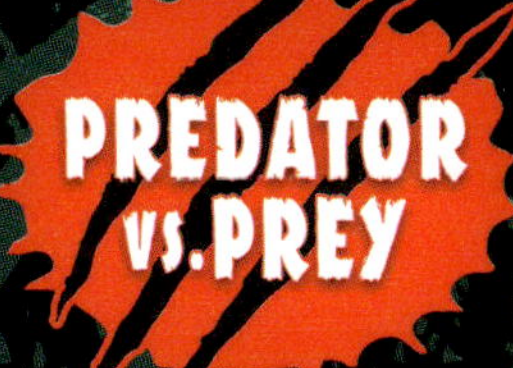

KILLER WHALES VS. PENGUINS

FOOD CHAIN FIGHTS

BEN HUBBARD

Lerner Publications ◆ Minneapolis

Lerner Publications Company
An imprint of Lerner Publishing Group, Inc.
241 First Avenue North
Minneapolis, MN 55401 USA

For reading levels and more information, look up this title at www.lernerbooks.com.

Main body text set in Aptifer Sans LT Pro.
Typeface provided by Linotype AG.

Editor: Nicole Berglund

Library of Congress Cataloging-in-Publication Data

Names: Hubbard, Ben, 1973– author.
Title: Killer whales vs. penguins : food chain fights / Ben Hubbard.
Description: Minneapolis : Lerner Publications, [2025] | Series: Predator vs. prey | Includes bibliographical references and index. | Audience: Ages 8–11 | Audience: Grades 2–3 | Summary: "Dive into the ocean where killer whales and penguins swim. Learn about each animal's strengths, weaknesses, defenses, attacks, and more. Then discover if predator or prey rules this habitat"— Provided by publisher.
Identifiers: LCCN 2024017955 (print) | LCCN 2024017956 (ebook) | ISBN 9798765647301 (library binding) | ISBN 9798765662144 (paperback) | ISBN 9798765656952 (epub)
Subjects: LCSH: Killer whale—Juvenile literature. | King penguin—Juvenile literature. | Killer whale—Antarctica—Juvenile literature. | King penguin—Antarctica—Juvenile literature. | Predation (Biology)—Juvenile literature.
Classification: LCC QL737.C432 H83 2025 (print) | LCC QL737.C432 (ebook) | DDC 599.53/6—dc23/eng/20240517

LC record available at https://lccn.loc.gov/2024017955
LC ebook record available at https://lccn.loc.gov/2024017956

Manufactured in the United States of America
2-1013333-53170-9/30/2025

TABLE OF CONTENTS

CHAPTER 1

MEET THE ANIMALS

IT IS MORNING IN THE COLD WATERS NEAR ANTARCTICA.
Hundreds of king penguins stand on an island shore. They watch one king penguin swim out. Suddenly, three black fins appear in the water. They are orcas, also called killer whales. The orcas slip below the surface behind the king penguin. But the penguin has seen them. The chase is on.

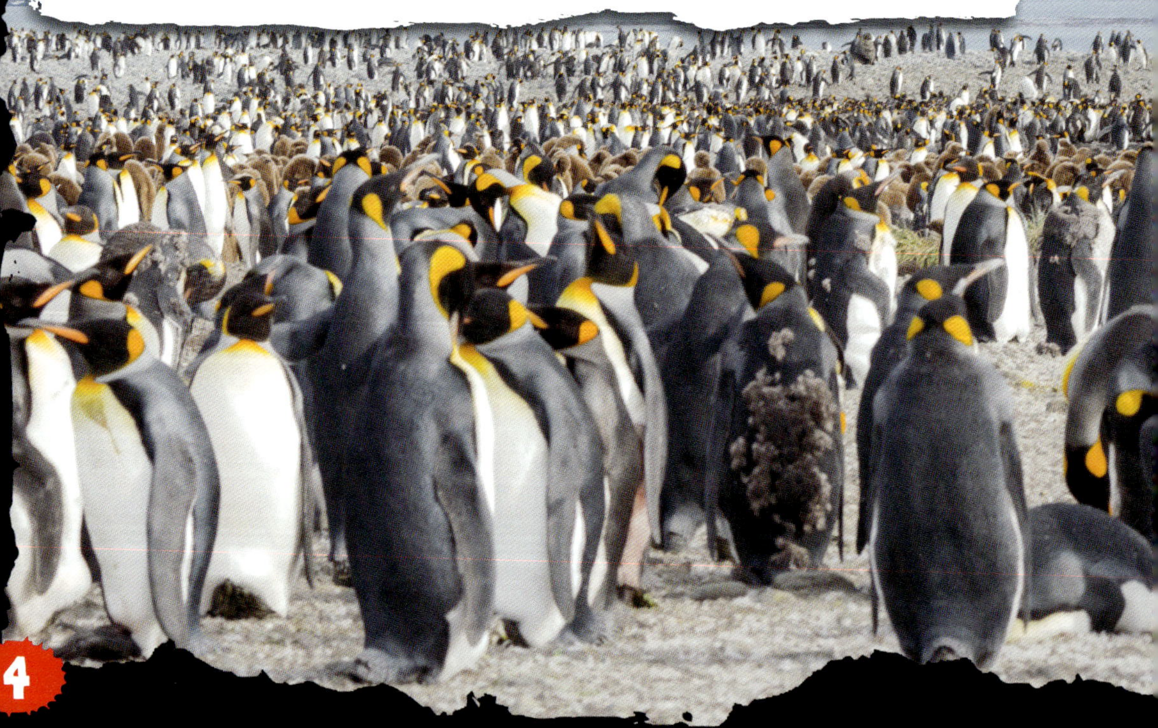

Orcas and king penguins share this chilly island habitat. Orcas prowl the island waters in packs. They are the top predator in the sea. Orcas hunt large prey, such as seals, sharks, and whales. They also hunt king penguins.

King penguins visit the islands to meet and mate. They stay mostly on the shore to breed. The penguins are safer on land. But adult penguins need to enter the sea to find fish for their young. This puts them in danger, though many king penguins survive orca attacks.

Orcas are large hunters that often eat king penguins. But king penguins are fast, agile, and hard to catch. The lone penguin twists and turns in the water. The orcas are right on its tail. The penguin sees an ice floe, or sheet, in the water. It speeds to jump onto the ice and escape.

Can the whales catch the penguin? Will it reach the ice in time? Which animal will win in this battle between predator and prey? Let's find out!

Orca pods, or groups, often consist of mother orcas and their offsping.

ORCA STATS

WEIGHT: up to 11 tons (9,979 kg)

LENGTH: up to 32 feet (9.8 m)

SWIMMING SPEED: up to 35 miles (56 km) per hour

KING PENGUIN STATS

WEIGHT: 31 to 37 pounds (14 to 16.8 kg)

LENGTH: 33 to 37 inches (83.8 to 94 cm)

SWIMMING SPEED: up to 7.6 miles (12.2 km) per hour

CHAPTER 2

ORCAS VS. KING PENGUINS

ORCAS AND KING PENGUINS HAVE MANY STRENGTHS AND SKILLS TO HELP THEM SURVIVE. But which would win in a battle? Let's compare them to see.

9

SIZE

Orcas are the largest members of the dolphin family. They are as heavy as two Asian elephants and as long as a school bus. Orcas have a dorsal fin on their back that is 3 to 6 feet (0.9 to 1.8 m) high. They also have large brains, weighing around 13.2 pounds (6 kg).

King penguins are the second-largest penguins. They are about as tall as a three-year-old human child. This makes them much smaller than orcas.

There are about eighteen different species of penguins.

SENSES

Orcas have excellent eyesight and hearing. They receive sound through their lower jawbone. They also have a special sense called echolocation. This sends high frequency sound waves into the water. When the sound waves hit an object, they bounce back. This tells the orca what is in front of it, even in deep, dark water.

King penguins have amazing eyes that are adapted to see on land and underwater. When they swim, their eyes let in more light. This means king penguins can see when they dive into deep, dark water. When they swim to the surface, their eyes let in less light so they can see in bright sunlight.

SPEED

Orcas have streamlined bodies for swimming at high speeds. They are one of the fastest creatures in the ocean. Most of the time, orcas cruise at around 5 miles (8 km) per hour. But when they hunt, orcas can reach a speed of 35 miles (56 km) per hour. This means they can usually outswim their prey.

OLD ORCAS

Female orcas can live up to one hundred years. Male orcas only live up to sixty years.

WING FLIPPERS

King penguins are birds with wings and feathers. But they cannot fly. Instead, they use their wings as flippers.

King penguins are much slower than orcas. They can only reach a speed of around 7.6 miles (12.2 km) per hour. But king penguins are much more agile than orcas. They can change direction quickly. This makes the penguins hard to catch!

A group of king penguins swims and hunts for food.

AGILITY

While orcas aren't as agile as penguins, they are agile for their size. They can even beach themselves on the shore to catch prey. They use waves to get back into the water. Orcas are also agile enough to jump out of the water. This is called breaching.

An orca breaching

King penguins can look clumsy on land. They waddle when they walk. But they are great swimmers. They use their wings as flippers to make tight turns. They also dive about 1,000 feet (305 m) and hold their breath for about thirty minutes. Orcas, on the other hand, come up to the surface to breathe every three to five minutes.

EGG WARMER

King penguins give birth by laying an egg. The parents take turns keeping the egg warm. While one parent stays with the egg, the other goes to the sea to fish.

COLORING

Orcas have a black back and a white belly. They also have a gray patch behind their dorsal fin. The orcas' color helps them hide their size. From above, their black back makes them hard to see in the dark water. From below, their white belly is hard to see against the sun. This can confuse other animals.

ORCAS EVERYWHERE

Orcas live in every sea and ocean in the world. They can be seen in tropical oceans but are found more often in the cold waters around Antarctica and Alaska.

King penguins are also white and black. Like orcas, their black backs make them hard to see from above. King penguins also have orange feathers on their cheeks, heads, and chests. King penguin chicks are covered in fluffy brown feathers.

About seventy feathers cover 1 square inch (6.5 sq. cm) of an adult king penguin's skin.

KEY WEAPONS

An orca's key weapons are its powerful jaws and teeth. Orcas have between forty and fifty-six cone-shaped teeth. Each tooth is around 3 inches (7.6 cm) long. Orcas bite down on their prey and rip off chunks of flesh. They swallow the chunks whole.

Orcas eat hundreds of pounds of food every day.

King penguins have sharp bills to hunt with. They grab prey such as fish and krill in their bills. The penguins have bristles on their tongues to help them grip prey and swallow. King penguins also defend themselves with the powerful muscles in their chest and flippers.

PROTECTING PENGUINS

King penguins must protect their eggs and chicks from hunting birds. These birds include giant petrels, skuas, and turkey vultures.

HUNTING HABITS

Orcas work as a team to catch prey. They have many hunting strategies. Sometimes, they blow bubbles into a school, or group, of fish to confuse them. Then the orcas eat them. Other times, orcas make waves by diving suddenly to knock prey off ice floes. Orcas also lift their heads out of the water to look for prey. This is called spy-hopping.

BREATH REMINDER

Orcas do not breathe automatically like humans. They have to remember to take a breath every time they need air.

King penguins are skilled hunters. They use their powerful flippers to swim fast after squid, lantern fish, and krill. They can make deep dives to catch fish. King penguins sometimes hunt krill in a pack. They swim around the krill to force the krill into a ball. Then they pick off the krill one by one.

Up to six hundred thousand king penguins can live together.

ATTACK AND DEFENSE STYLES

Orcas have several ways to attack. Sometimes, they use their powerful tails to hit large prey, such as great white sharks. This stuns the prey so the orca can eat it. Orcas ram prey such as smaller whales with their hard snout. They then eat certain parts and leave the remains for scavengers.

Orcas have a layer of fat called blubber to keep them warm.

King penguins have several ways to defend themselves. They often swim near the water's surface where there are small waves. The waves can confuse predators. The penguins then dive down deep and out of sight. King penguins can also leap high out of the water and onto land. This is called porpoising.

PROTECTED BY FAT

King penguins are covered with a layer of fat under their skin. They can survive for over fifty days without eating.

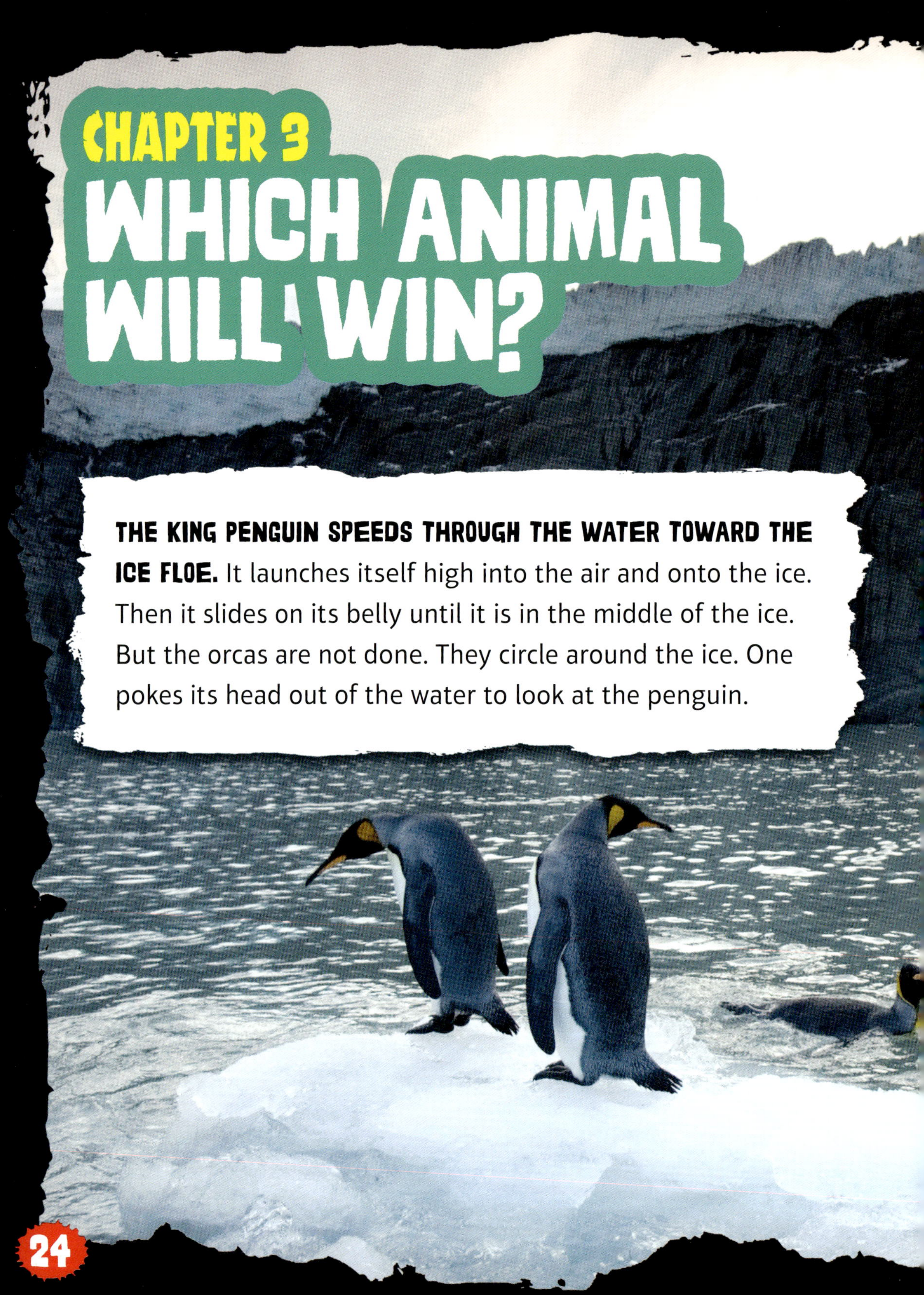

CHAPTER 3

WHICH ANIMAL WILL WIN?

THE KING PENGUIN SPEEDS THROUGH THE WATER TOWARD THE ICE FLOE. It launches itself high into the air and onto the ice. Then it slides on its belly until it is in the middle of the ice. But the orcas are not done. They circle around the ice. One pokes its head out of the water to look at the penguin.

King penguins rest on ice floes.

The king penguin cannot hold on. It slips from the ice floe into the water. An orca then rams the penguin with its snout. Another orca grabs it in its jaws. The penguin is gone. From the shore, other penguins watch. Today the orcas got a meal. They are the top predator of this ocean habitat.

An orca hunts a king penguin.

King penguins can live about twenty-six years in the wild.

RULER OF THE HABITAT

Orcas are strong animals with big brains. They work together to catch their prey. But they do not always win in the race for survival. King penguins have special skills and strengths of their own. They are agile and speedy, and have excellent eyesight. This means they often escape orcas. But who knows what will happen tomorrow? Every day is different in the fight for survival. Sometimes, the prey wins, and other times, the predator.

PREDATOR VS. PREY: HEAD-TO-HEAD

ORCA

- Between forty and fifty-six cone-shaped teeth
- Powerful nose and tail to ram and stun prey

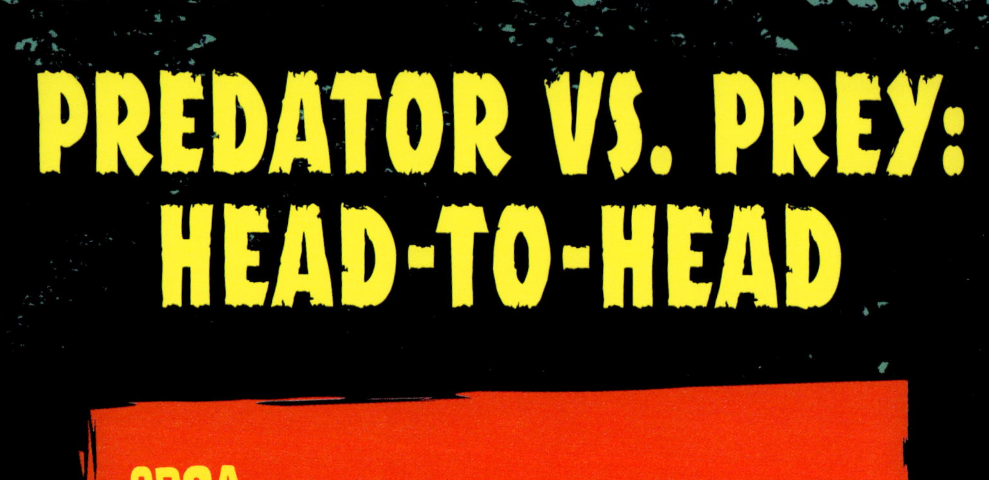

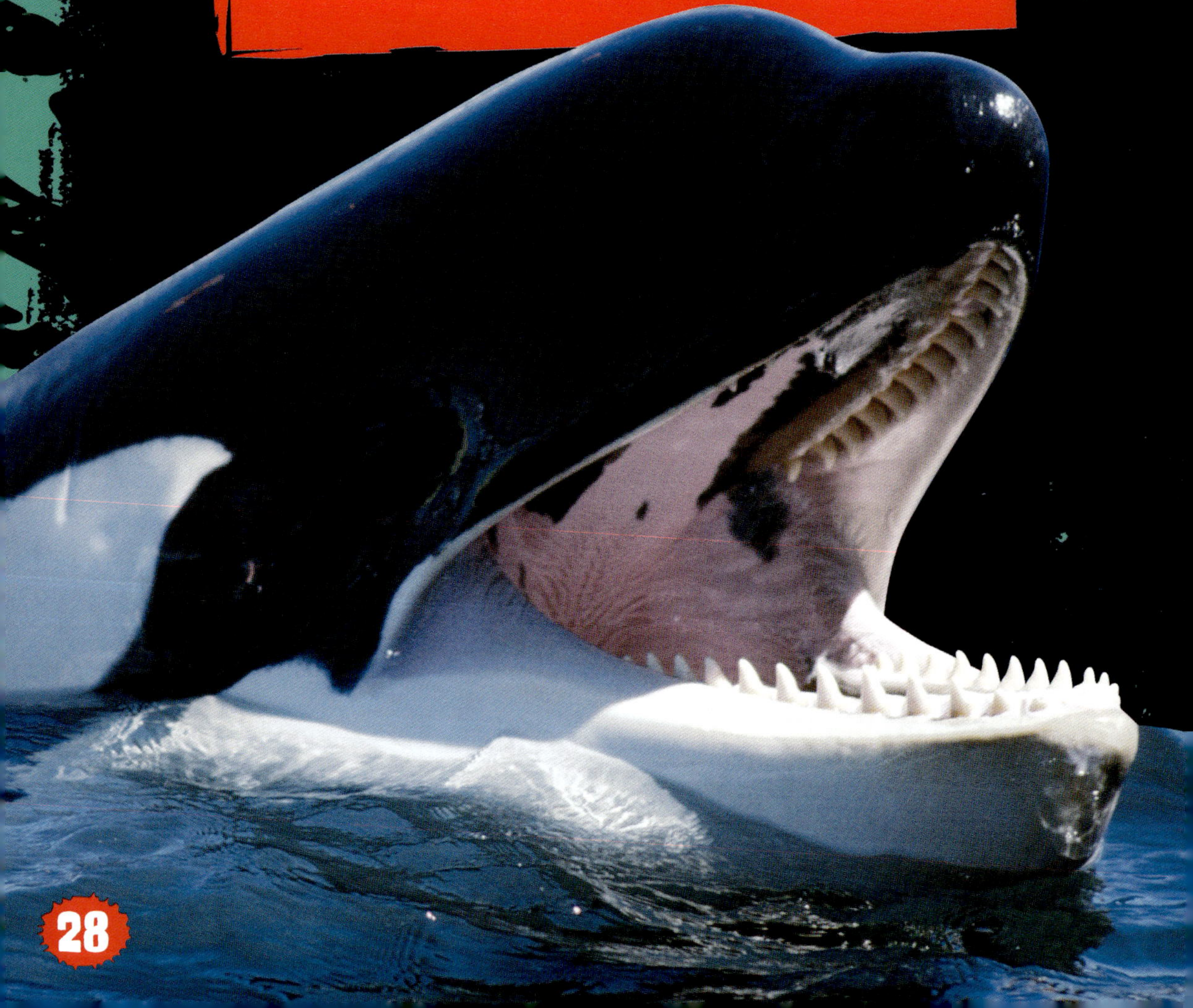

KING PENGUIN
• Powerful flippers for speedy swimming and deep dives
• Sharp bill to grab prey and fend off predators
29

GLOSSARY

agile: able to move quickly and easily

beach: leap onto the edge of the shore from the water

habitat: the home of an animal or plant

ice floe: a sheet of ice floating in the water

krill: tiny, shell-covered sea creatures

predator: an animal that hunts and kills other animals for food

prey: an animal that is hunted and killed for food by a predator

sense: the way an animal understands its surroundings, including touch, smell, taste, sight, and hearing

skua: a large, hunting seabird related to seagulls

streamlined: shaped to move easily through water

waddle: walking with short steps, like a duck

LEARN MORE

Britannica Kids: Killer Whale
https://kids.britannica.com/kids/article/killer-whale/574601

Britannica Kids: Penguin
https://kids.britannica.com/kids/article/penguin/353611

Hubbard, Ben. *Great White Sharks vs. Dolphins: Food Chain Fights.* Minneapolis: Lerner Publications, 2025.

National Geographic Kids: Orca
https://kids.nationalgeographic.com/animals/mammals/facts/orca

Schuh, Mari C. *Penguins*. Minneapolis: Jump!, 2024.

Wilson, Sierra. *Orca*. New York: Lightbox Learning, 2023.

INDEX

PHOTO ACKNOWLEDGMENTS

Jose Gieskes/Getty Images, pp. 4–5; ©2020 GEOSTOCK/Getty Images, p. 6; Musat/Getty Images, p. 7 (top); Mint Images - David Schultz/Getty Images, p. 7 (bottom); wildestanimal/Getty Images, pp. 8–9; Alexey_Seafarer/Getty Images, p. 10; Grafissimo/Getty Images, p. 11; Frank Kaiser/Getty Images, p. 12; Kevin Schafer/Getty Images, p. 13; Wirestock/Getty Images, p. 14; Paul Souders/Getty Images, pp. 15, 21; Nature Picture Library/Alamy, p. 16; charliebishop/Getty Images, p. 17; Musat/Getty Images, p. 18; Danita Delimont/Alamy, p. 19; Ron Sanford/Getty Images, p. 20; Poelzer Wolfgang/Alamy, p. 22; All Canada Photos/Alamy, p. 23; Danita Delimont Creative/Alamy, pp. 24–25; © Ian McCarthy /NPL/Minden Pictures, p. 26; Enrique Aguirre Aves/Getty Images, p. 27; Jeff Foott/Getty Images, p. 28; Danita Delimont/Getty Images, p. 29. Design elements: iunewind/Shutterstock; Milano M/Shutterstock; Cassel/Shutterstock; Textures and backgrounds/Shutterstock; Print Net/Shutterstock; Ukrainian studio/Shutterstock.

Cover: Grafissimo/Getty Images (whale); Paul A. Souders/Getty Images (penguin).